True TEEN Stories

SCHOLASTIC INC.

New York Toronto London Auckland Sydney
Mexico City New Delhi Hong Kong Buenos Aires

"No More Lies" adapted from "Growing Up Multiracial" by Laura D'Angelo from *Scholastic Action*, September 17, 2001. Copyright © 2001 by Scholastic Inc. All rights reserved.

Adapted from "Dying to Be Thin" by John DiConsiglio from *Scholastic Choices*, November/December 2000. Copyright © 2000 by Scholastic Inc. All rights reserved.

Adapted from "After the Crash" by Robin Landew Silverman from *Scholastic Scope*, October 18, 1999. Copyright © 1999 by Scholastic Inc. All rights reserved.
"What's Your Safe-Driving IQ?" from *Scholastic Scope*, March 8, 1999.
Copyright © 1999 by Scholastic Inc. All rights reserved.

"Escaping Death" by John Kuol, as told to Karen Fanning, from *Scholastic Scope*, September 3, 2001. Copyright © 2001 by Scholastic Inc. All rights reserved.

Adapted from "Bullying Really Hurts" by John DiConsiglio from *Scholastic Action*, September 3, 2001. Copyright © 2001 by Scholastic Inc. All rights reserved.
Adapted from "A Bully Apologizes" by Denise Rinaldo from *Scholastic Choices*, October 2001. Copyright © 2001 by Scholastic Inc. All rights reserved.

2   3   4   5   6   7   8   9   10   23   10   09   08   07   06   05   04

Contents

Daniel de la Cruz, center, with (from left to right) his sister, Jessica, his mom, Angela, and his brother, Gabriel.

1 No More Lies

By Laura D'Angelo

Today, when Daniel de la Cruz glances in the mirror, he sees an 18-year-old with a richly diverse ethnic heritage: Cuban, Mexican, Native American, and Irish. Yet, when others look at him, they simply see a young black man. The difference between these two images hasn't always been easy for Daniel.

Daniel was born in Los Angeles six minutes before his twin sister, Jessica. She has light olive skin, a freckled face, straight jet-black hair, and closely resembles her Mexican father. Daniel has darker skin and looks like his mother, who is Cuban, Native American, and Irish. When Daniel and Jessica were growing up, strangers would often stare at them, unable to believe that the pair could possibly be twins.

"I used to tell Jessica that she had it so easy," Daniel says. "In this society, she could go to an all-white country club and nobody would look twice. I'd probably be asked to leave."

For Daniel's mother, this difference in the twins' physical appearance and the difficulty it caused was a chronic source of anxiety. "I felt sad knowing that this would become a lifelong issue between them," she says.

PHOTO: TOD BIGELOW

Choosing To Be Latino

As Daniel grew older, he started asking himself: Where do I fit in? How should I dress? How should I act? Should I learn more Spanish and hang with the Latinos? Should I use the same slang words as the black kids do?

When Daniel enrolled at a Catholic boys' high school in Los Angeles, he felt that his choice would now be clear. "Since the population was mostly Latino, I felt pressure to be a part of them. I felt I had to prove myself more because my skin was darker," he says. However, Daniel's attempts to belong backfired painfully. The Latino students were far more fluent in Spanish than Daniel was, and they mocked his struggles to speak the language. His inability to communicate in Spanish left him outside their social circle.

Daniel was becoming more troubled and confused about his identity than ever. Eventually, he began to dread school. He began to cut classes, and soon, he started skipping school altogether.

Choosing To Be Black

Daniel got the opportunity for a fresh start in 10th grade, at a public high school in Los Angeles. One day, a group of black girls were skipping rope and invited Daniel to join them. Later, some boys invited him to play a pick-up game of basketball.

Daniel was heartened by their friendliness. "They seemed nice and I thought they'd be accepting," he remembers. He kept his Latin side concealed so his new friends wouldn't reject him. The school was predominately

Mexican and black, and relations between the two groups were sometimes tense.

More and more, Daniel's new friends included him in their activities. They even took him shopping for clothes, advising him on fashion matters—where to get the right sneakers, extra-wide-leg jeans, bright T-shirts, and a duffel bag. Daniel appreciated their efforts and jumped at the chance to belong. "I wished I was darker and could talk like the other guys to complete the image," he says.

All Alone

The makeover didn't exactly turn out how Daniel had expected. Pretty soon, Daniel's new clothes made him feel ashamed of himself. He realized that his new clothes were nothing more than a disguise, and he did not feel comfortable in them. "I thought, 'I can't *believe* the lengths I would go to just to be accepted,'" he says. "I felt like a fake."

Still desperate to fit in, Daniel felt pressured to conform to the crowd. Fearing rejection, he even betrayed his Latino roots by joining his friends when they made fun of the Mexican students. Then one day, he accidentally let a Spanish word slip out and knew instantly that his ruse was over. "I thought I had ruined everything," he says. "I felt like crying."

The rejection Daniel feared was not just paranoia; it was reality. A few weeks later, his new girlfriend abruptly dumped him. She called him a racist name for a Mexican, and the slur wounded him deeply.

After that, Daniel ate alone in the cafeteria, questioning whether he would ever find acceptance. "I kept thinking about what had happened and what I could have done differently. Then I thought, 'I should embrace who I am. Just because I can't prove who I am to others, doesn't mean I shouldn't be happy,'" he says.

No More Lies

One day, a Mexican girl invited Daniel to sit with her and her friends during school. Daniel was grateful to be included but was also guarded. "I wanted to be accepted, but I didn't want to feel like I had to lie about myself," he says.

Daniel used to feel ashamed about his multiracial background. Now he's learned to embrace it with pride.

Finally, Daniel decided to reveal his secret and told the Mexican kids about his multiracial heritage. He explained that his life-long dream was to visit Cuba, a country whose people have a wide variety of skin colors. "Some are dark and some are light," Daniel says. "But there's not as much prejudice. People thought my dream was cool and that I was exotic."

Proud of His Heritage

Today, Daniel is a senior at his high school, splitting his time between 12th grade and a city college. He has worked hard academically and blossomed socially, but Daniel had some help. He credits a support group called Multiracial Americans of Southern California (MASC) with providing a place where he was able to feel totally accepted and comfortable with himself. In fact, Daniel is so involved with the group that he has plans to run for president of MASC.

As a result of feeling more comfortable with himself, Daniel also has developed a much closer relationship with his sister, Jessica. "We fight, but deep down, we're close," he says. Daniel now realizes that even though Jessica's appearance is different from his, she, too, shares his struggle to be accepted.

Daniel is anxious to help others who are still having a hard time. "It hasn't been easy for me," says Daniel. "I want to let other kids know what it took me a long time to figure out: Be proud of yourself, and let people know who you are."

What does it mean to be multiracial or biracial?

Like Daniel, children whose parents come from many different races often refer to themselves as multiracial, mixed race, or racially mixed. Children whose parents are from two different races—such as Hispanic and black—often refer to themselves as biracial.

How many people are multiracial or biracial in the United States?

The number of people who come from racially mixed backgrounds has skyrocketed in the past few decades. During the late 1960s, the U.S. Supreme Court overturned the last laws barring interracial marriage. After that, the number of mixed race marriages has exploded by 800 percent. From 1970 to 1990, the number of multiracial children quadrupled to 2 million, according to the U.S. Census Bureau. Among them are celebrities like Tiger Woods and Derek Jeter. And they are important role models for the next generation. Today, there are at least 4 million racially mixed children in the U.S. who are 18 years old or younger.

What are the biggest challenges that mixed-race teenagers face?

From an early age, many racially mixed kids learn that others perceive them and their families as being different—or worse. They know this because of the way people stare at them or act towards them. Many multiracial teens have experienced the painful effects of discrimination and racism first hand. Sometimes the racism comes from the very groups to which they feel they belong.

What can be done to fight prejudice and racism?

As Martin Luther King Jr. said, we should judge people by "the content of their character," not their skin color, sex, or religion. Try to resist the temptation to label people. Try to appreciate them for their individual qualities, such as humor, honesty, kindness, intelligence, bravery, and creativity. Help others do the same. There are other steps you can take as well. If someone tells a racist joke, don't laugh. When someone uses a racial slur, don't encourage it. Make it clear that this kind behavior is simply not cool.

The United States is more diverse today than it's ever been. The pie chart below shows how people identify themselves. These are the different flavors of the American pie, in the year 2000.

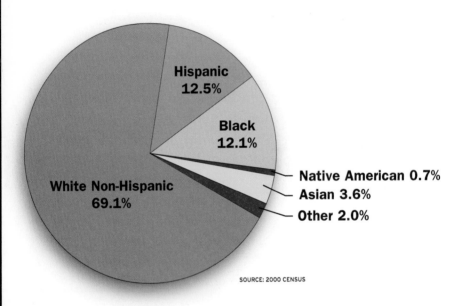

Hispanic 12.5%

Black 12.1%

Native American 0.7%
Asian 3.6%
Other 2.0%

White Non-Hispanic 69.1%

SOURCE: 2000 CENSUS

Answer the questions, according to the information given in the pie chart.

• What are the groups in order from the largest to the smallest?

• Which two groups are nearly the same size?

• In which category would persons of mixed raced be likely to place themselves?

Take a poll in your class and create a pie chart like the one above. How close are your results to the ones shown here?

What are your roots? On a separate piece of paper, make a family tree like the one below. Write the names of the countries (or U.S. cities) where your relatives or caregivers were born, and try to fill as many boxes as you can. You may need to get information from family records and/or relatives. If you are Native American, try to find out the regions of America where your ancestors originally lived.

FAMILY TREE

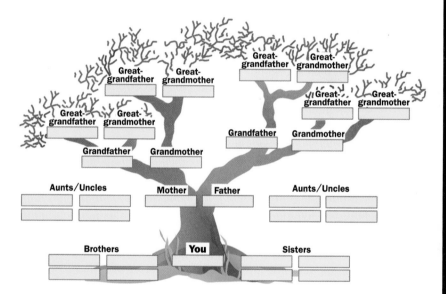

Great-grandfather Great-grandmother

Great-grandfather Great-grandmother

Great-grandfather Great-grandmother

Great-grandfather Great-grandmother

Grandfather Grandmother

Grandfather Grandmother

Aunts/Uncles   Mother   Father   Aunts/Uncles

Brothers   **You**   Sisters

Research Tip

After you've collected information from your family, you may want to check out www.ellisislandrecords.org. This Web site will let you look up immigrants' names, ages, places of origin, and arrival dates. But be careful. Ellis Island was famous for creative spelling of names!

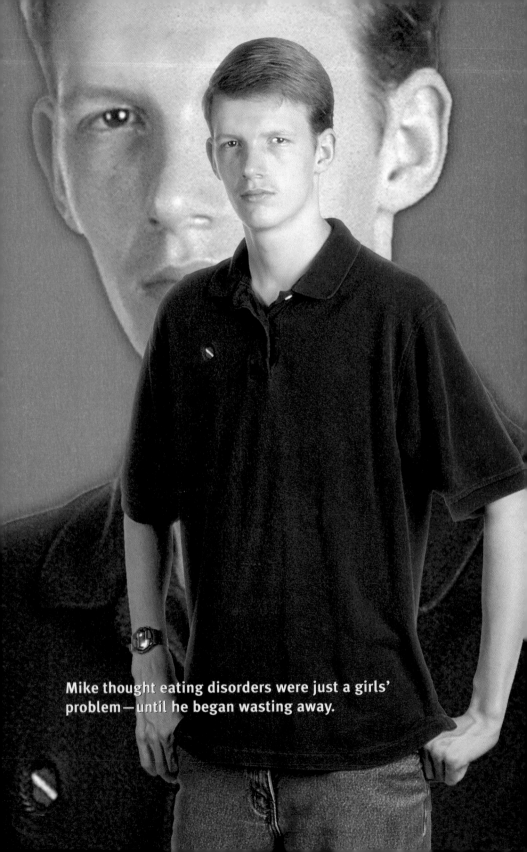
Mike thought eating disorders were just a girls' problem—until he began wasting away.

2 Dying to be Thin

by John DiConsiglio

For Mike Rogerson, the wake-up call of his life came in the middle of an otherwise ordinary school day. He was suddenly asked to go to the library. Mike, 15, was certain that he had no overdue books. What could be important enough to drag him out of class?

Swinging open the library doors of his Florida school, Mike was astonished to see his best friend, Tom Wilson, and three of his favorite teachers seated around a table. At first, Mike thought he was in trouble or that something had happened to his family. But his English teacher quickly patted Mike's shoulder reassuringly and said, "Mike, something is going on with you. I think you have an eating disorder, and you're not leaving this library until you get help."

"Are you crazy?" Mike said. "Girls get eating disorders. Not guys." His defiance and anger were escalating by the minute. He couldn't believe what he was hearing—even though deep down he had to admit something was terribly wrong.

In the space of a month, he'd lost more than 50 pounds from his 6-foot 5-inch frame—dropping from 214 pounds to 160. Mike's relationship to food had become distorted and harmful. In other words, Mike had an eating disorder. But, he didn't realize it because, like most people, Mike believed that anorexia was a female problem.

Although most people with eating disorders are female, more and more males also are afflicted. According to a new study, one in six eating-disorder victims are men or boys. In total, that means more than 1 million males in the U.S. are battling the disease—the majority of whom, experts say, are athletes struggling to control their weight for competition.

"Eating disorders in men aren't well understood. And to an extent, they aren't taken very seriously," says Vivian Hanson Meehan, R.N., founder of the National Association of Anorexia Nervosa and Associated Disorders (ANAD). "Many men deny they have an eating disorder," she says. "It's hard to get them to accept help."

Denying the Problem

That day in the library, Mike wasn't aware of his problem or looking for help, though his friend Tom and teachers were very worried about him. He was exercising incessantly–running three miles a day with weighted garbage bags taped beneath his sweatpants. He was throwing away his lunch every day.

"I insisted there was nothing wrong with me," says Mike, now 20. "I was just dropping a few pounds for wrestling. I told them I'd be over it in a week or two."

Sadly, Mike was wrong. He is still struggling to overcome his eating disorder—though he has been under a psychotherapist's and medical doctor's care for more than five years. As a result of this disease, his weight has dropped as low as 127 pounds.

Mike's eating disorder began with bulimia—he would binge on massive amounts of food and then "purge" by throwing it up or using laxatives and diuretics to force his body to eliminate it. Now Mike is anorexic—he deprives himself of food almost completely, fasting for as long as a month at a time.

Mike's inability to eat has not only given a skeletal look to his body, it has also caused massive internal damage. A healthy weight includes a certain percentage of body fat. The kidneys, liver, and other organs need fat to function. Mike's eating disorder has robbed his body of the necessary fat, leaving his kidneys and liver badly damaged. Purging has deprived his body of the mineral potassium. A lack of potassium can lead to heart failure— the prime cause of death among people with eating disorders. Indeed, a lack of fat and potassium has caused Mike's heart to shrink.

Feeling Worthless

Experts believe that eating disorders almost always contain some emotional component. In therapy, Mike examined the roots of his own problem. He felt certain that a bad relationship with his father contributed to the development of his disorder.

"He was verbally abusive toward me," Mike says. "He's a harsh guy. He was always calling me fat and lazy. He would tell me I'd never amount to much in life." Mike

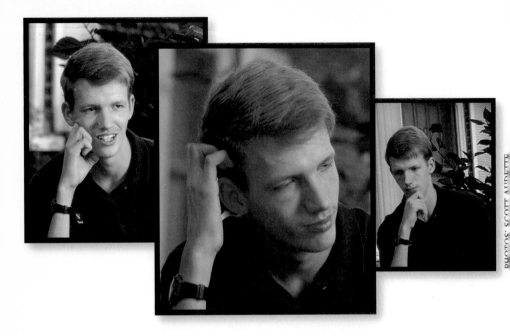

Though he is clearly very thin, Mike Rogerson sees a fat person when he looks in the mirror.

was an A student, but despite his academic achievements, he felt worthless. To please his dad, he went out for the wrestling team.

"I'm tall, so I weighed over 200 pounds," Mike says. "But all the other guys in my weight class were made of muscle. I knew I couldn't compete with them." Mike decided he had to drop enough weight to qualify for a lighter weight class, where he felt he'd have a better chance.

Mike started an intense workout regime, but when he failed to lose enough weight, he began vomiting meals. Soon he was caught up in a cycle of binging and purging. He would eat enormous quantities of food, downing hamburgers as if they were crackers. Then, when he was alone, Mike forced himself to vomit it all back up.

"I thought it was just temporary, until I made the weight," Mike says. "But when I made the weight, I was so weak that I couldn't wrestle."

That's when his friends and teachers cornered Mike in the library. A few days later, Mike began spitting up blood in the middle of history class. His constant forced vomiting had ravaged the lining of his stomach. His mom rushed him to a doctor, who delivered sobering news.

"He told me that what I was doing would eventually kill me," Mike says.

Tough Road Back

Terrified by the doctor's prognosis, Mike finally agreed that he needed help. Eating disorders can be treated, and most cases are not as severe as Mike's. The most successful treatment, experts say, combines therapy to heal the psychological wounds and food reeducation to teach sufferers how to eat healthy again. Mike has had some victories, but he has suffered many setbacks, as well. For a while he got his weight up to nearly 160, but after a recent relapse, his weight dropped back to 137.

The worst part of the disease, Mike says, is the loneliness. "No one understands this," he says. "Every day, from the moment I wake up to the time I go to bed, I think about this. This isn't a normal life."

Still, Mike hasn't given up hope. The courage he has shown in facing his problem and his willingness to accept help may ultimately be his greatest weapons. "Right now, I'm focusing on staying alive," he says. "And every day that I'm still here gives me another day to fight."

Are You At Risk?

If you think you or a friend may have an eating disorder, you're not alone. Experts estimate that as many as 8 million Americans —male and female combined—suffer from anorexia or bulimia. Teens are especially vulnerable; 90 percent of those with an eating disorder start to get sick before age 20.

Below are some warning signs that could indicate that you have an unhealthy relationship with food. Read the list and check any item that describes you. If you check one or more, you may have a problem—but don't panic. Discuss your concerns with a trusted adult, school counselor, or doctor.

- You weigh yourself frequently and feel hideously fat no matter how many pounds you lose.

- You sneak food or lie about your eating habits.

- You don't like to eat in front of other people and skip social events because you know food will be served.

- You starve yourself for a day or more, then overeat and hate yourself for being weak.

- You purge by vomiting or using laxatives, or you exercise for hours a day even though your team or coach does not require it.

For More Information

If you need help with an eating disorder, if you want to help a friend, or if you just want information, contact the Eating Disorders Awareness and Prevention referral hot line at 800-931-2231. Or, visit the group's Web site: www.edap.org

Think the wispy thin models and actors you see in magazines or on TV are just born lucky? Then think again. As you're about to read, being superstar thin can come at a dangerous price, even for the most glamorous of stars.

Chistina Ricci Remembered as the skinny little girl from *The Addams Family,* Ricci developed a voluptuous figure as she matured. Ashamed of it, she became anorexic. She says, "I still don't think I'm thin enough to succeed, but I don't want to be thin enough."

Daniel Johns At the height of his band's success, Silverchair frontman Johns developed anorexia. His hit "Ana's Song" was inspired by his struggle. "I haven't recovered, but I think I've hit my lowest point and I'm only on my way up," he says.

Elisa Donovan While playing the fashion-obsessed Amber on *Clueless,* Donovan was obsessing over her weight in real life. Anorexic for two years—living on coffee, water, and grapes—she sought help after having heart palpitations. Now, she says, "I'm getting more comfortable with my body and won't allow anorexia to define who I am."

PHOTOS: SCOTT AUDETTE

The average teenage boy needs 2,800 calories a day to maintain a healthy weight. Teenage girls need 2,200 calories a day. To eat a healthy diet, the United States Department of Agriculture (USDA) recommends you follow the food pyramid guidelines. On a separate piece of paper, write a healthy menu for one day. See if you can meet the daily nutritional requirement for each group and stay within your calorie range.

❶ Fats, Oils, and Sweets
(use sparingly)

- butter, 1 tbsp. (110)
- jam or jelly, 1 tbsp. (55)
- mayonnaise, 1 tbsp. (110)
- ice cream, 1/2 cup vanilla (135)
- potato chips, 10 (105)
- chocolate bar (220)
- cola, 1 can (152)
- salad dressing, 1 tbsp. (65)

❷ Milk, Yogurt, and Cheese
(2–3 servings a day)

- whole milk, 1 cup (160)
- chocolate milk, 1 cup (190)
- yogurt, 1 cup (120)
- processed American cheese, 2 slices (140)
- cheddar cheese, 4 diced cubes (280)
- cottage cheese, 1/2 cup (101)

❸ Meat, Poultry, Fish, Dry Beans, Eggs, and Nuts
(2–3 servings a day)

- eggs, 2 medium (214)
- small hamburger, 3 oz. (250)
- cashews, 6 to 8 (88)
- peanut butter, 2 tbsp. (190)
- fried chicken, 3 oz. (155)
- dry beans and peas, cooked, 1/2 cup (140)
- fish filet (Halibut), broiled, 3 oz. (155)

❹ Vegetables
(3–5 servings a day)

- tomato, 1/2 cup (35)
- lettuce, 1 cup (10)
- baked potato, small (90)
- french fries, 10 medium (155)
- green beans, 1 cup cooked (30)
- carrots, 1/2 cup (25)

❺ Fruits
(2–4 servings a day)

- apple, 1 medium (70)
- banana, 1 medium (85)
- orange, 1 medium (60)
- canned fruit cocktail, 1/2 cup (97)
- avocado, 1/4 whole (92)

❻ Bread, Cereal, Rice, and Pasta
(6–11 servings a day)

- white bread, 1 slice (60)
- wheat bread, 1 slice (55)
- hamburger roll, 1 medium (89)
- rice, cooked, 1/2 cup (93)
- pasta, cooked, 1/2 cup (100)
- cereal, 1/2 cup (120)
- doughnut, 1 medium (125)
- cookies, 2 medium (240)

With neither a driver's license nor a worry, Nikki Arden got behind the wheel one day when she was 15. It was a drive that ended two lives—and changed hers forever.

3 After the Crash

by Robin Landew Silverman

Nikki Arden will never forget May 2, 1994. The sun was shining, the sky was blue, and a warm spring breeze beckoned for her to be outside.

Earlier that day, she and her friend Ann* had hatched a plan to skip their afternoon classes at Greenway High School. They had decided that they needed to cheer themselves up after reminiscing about a friend who'd died in a snowmobile accident during the winter. The conversation had left them both feeling melancholy.

"We asked another friend if we could borrow her Jeep Cherokee so we could just drive around," Nikki said. The girl entrusted them with the keys. Although neither Nikki nor Ann had even a learner's permit, they headed out onto a two-lane road in Nashwauk, Minnesota. Ann drove first. Then Nikki, who had celebrated her 15th birthday just the day before, slid behind the wheel.

Driving Toward Disaster

Several miles away, Bernice Foley, 56, was driving her mother, Marguerite Robbins, 76, to a rummage sale.

* name has been changed

Marguerite loved collectibles; every shelf of her cozy farmhouse was laden with the treasures she'd unearthed. The mother of 16 children, grandmother of 53, and great-grandmother of 70, Marguerite was a bundle of spirit and energy, her age notwithstanding. Relatives were always stopping by for a visit—and to savor the pies, cookies, and cakes she baked every morning. When she wasn't cooking or canning, Marguerite was likely to be out feeding the animals—including nine black bears—that roamed through her yard.

Marguerite's passion for life was shared by her daughter Bernice, who had six children and six grandchildren of her own, and worked at a nearby nursing home. Despite her hectic schedule, Bernice spent hours driving her mother wherever she wanted to go. Ever since Marguerite's mother was tragically killed by a teen driver in 1964, Marguerite had refused to get the behind the wheel.

Four Lives Collide

As they motored down the highway, Nikki and Ann were not paying much attention to the road; they were busy laughing and goofing around. "Suddenly, I pulled to the right," Nikki remembers. The Jeep Cherokee swerved off the road onto the gravel shoulder. Nikki panicked. "I overcorrected, and I don't remember what happened after that," she says.

According to the police report, the Jeep lurched back onto the road, crossed the line, and crashed head-on into the pickup truck driven by Bernice. The pickup truck plunged into a culvert, and the crash was so severe that the vehicle was unrecognizable.

The Jeep was also totaled, and Nikki and Ann, who were wearing their seat belts, were knocked out by the impact, but they both survived. Nikki regained consciousness first. "Ann was making noises like she was choking, and I thought I remembered from my lifesaving classes that she could be choking on her tongue, so I lifted her head up," Nikki says. "But [a paramedic] yelled at me not to touch her in case there was a neck injury." Nikki was badly bruised, but she was able to walk to the ambulance while Ann was carried to another ambulance on a stretcher.

At the hospital, the police questioned Nikki about the accident. Doctors had already run a blood-alcohol test on her, and the results showed she had not been drinking. When the hospital-appointed therapist told her that the occupants of the other car were dead, Nikki began to cry uncontrollably.

Nikki couldn't believe that in one careless instant behind the wheel she could devastate so many lives—including her own. But the sad truth is that Nikki's story is far from unique. Although teen drivers represent only about two percent of all motorists in this country, they cause more than ten percent of all car crashes. In the year 2000, an estimated 4,869 teens died in car accidents, another 569,000 were injured, and 3,942 other motorists were killed, according the National Highway Traffic Safety Administration. Tragically, that day, Nikki had just added to the human wreckage left behind by inexperienced teen driving.

The victims: Bernice Foley (second from left) and Marguerite Robbins (far right).

Taking the Blame

Nikki was well enough to go home that night, and Ann was released from the hospital with minor injuries a day later. The next morning, when what Nikki had done really began to sink in, her feelings of guilt and shame were overwhelming. "When I first woke up, I thought it had all been a really bad dream," she says. "As I went through the day, I kept feeling that it would have been better if I had been the one who died."

Although she didn't say much to her family about the accident, she quickly became consumed with self-hate. "You deserve to die in a car accident as punishment," she told herself over and over. As the days passed, Nikki's mother, Darcy, grew more and more concerned for her daughter. Fearful of the hostile reaction her daughter might get from her classmates, Darcy and her husband, Rick, suggested that Nikki remain home from school and finish out the academic year with a tutor.

But Nikki refused steadfastly. "I was scared to go back to school, but I wanted to be with my friends," she says. While most of her classmates and teachers were thoughtful and supportive, others were not. "One of my friend's sisters called me a murderer," she says. "At the time, I just pretended I didn't hear it, but I knew that it was true. I thought about what I'd done all the time."

Coping With Grief

Meanwhile, about 65 miles away, Joan Wirtz, daughter of Marguerite Robbins and sister of Bernice Foley, was grappling with her own anguish and disbelief. She had already suffered a crushing loss. Joan's son, Ricky, had been killed in a freak explosion at work just five months earlier, and she was still mourning his untimely death. With her mother and sister gone, Joan's rage intensified.

"What did I do to deserve losing three loved ones like that, in such a short span and so violently?" she asks. "I vowed I would hate Nikki until my dying day."

The breaking point for Joan came at her mother and sister's funeral. "I remember walking out of there and my legs just starting to shake," she says. "I ran to the bathroom, and my good friend Edna came in to comfort me. I was sitting on the floor crying like an idiot, and she said, 'Just cry.'"

Joan was still seething with anger when she came to court to attend Nikki's sentencing before the juvenile authorities two months later. Because Nikki had already pleaded guilty, there was no trial. This would be the first time Joan would come face-to-face with the person who killed two of the dearest people in her family, and as she waited for the proceedings to begin, she struggled to keep her emotions under control.

"I remember thinking, When that girl arrives, what am I gonna do? Am I going to say something to her? Am I going to tell her, 'I hate you'?" But when Nikki walked into the room sobbing, Joan's anger suddenly dissipated.

"She was crying and she was scared to death. She was so young; it was just horrible," Joan recalls. "I felt sad for her, because she was so crushed. I sat there looking at her thinking, 'This poor kid—what she has to go through for the rest of her life. This could have been one of my kids.' Suddenly, I just didn't hate her anymore."

For Joan, the relief was profound and immediate. "It was like a weight lifted off my shoulders," Joan says. "I didn't have that hatred in my soul."

During the hearing, Nikki couldn't compose herself and stop crying. "I'm so sorry for what I've done," she told the judge. Nikki was sentenced to probation, until she was 18. She was also required to get counseling, to put flowers on the graves of her victims three times a year, and to write a letter to Marguerite and Bernice's family apologizing for what she'd done.

Learning to Forgive

In May 1995, one year after the crash, Nikki called Joan and asked if she would meet her and show her Marguerite's and Bernice's graves. Joan was stunned. "I never thought she would do it. I thought, 'They're not going to force this kid to put flowers on a grave. She's going to say she did and they're simply going to take her word for it.'"

Hearing Nikki's voice made Joan recall how scared the teenager had been on the day of the hearing. "I asked how she was doing," Joan says. "And she said, 'I still have a long way to go.'"

Joan met with Nikki and Darcy at the cemetery a week later. Tears cascaded down the teenager's cheeks as she stepped out of her mother's car and walked haltingly toward the graves of the two women, two red roses in hand. Says Joan, "I really don't think Nikki realized the extent of what she'd done, until that morning."

As she knelt and placed the flowers against the headstones, Nikki was overcome with remorse. "This should be me," she said. "I'm the one who deserved to die."

Joan stood by Nikki's side and began to sob quietly. Nikki's tears began to well up again, too. She turned to Joan. "I am so sorry," she said. Joan gave Nikki a hug and said, "You don't know how much pain you've caused us, but you're young and you have your future ahead of you. Learn from it. Go on. Make a life."

Vowing to Never Forget

"Knowing Joan had forgiven me helped me to forgive myself," Nikki says. Before they left the cemetery that day, she gave Joan a rose and a card with a packet of forget-me-not seeds.

Today, at 20, Nikki works for an insurance company in Virginia Beach, Virginia. "I'm more responsible now," she says. "I think about how what I do is going to affect others. I've become strong in my faith, leaning on God for a lot."

But the horrible memory of May 2, 1994 is indelibly burned into her mind. "I have a picture of [Bernice and Marguerite's] grave sites on the mirror in my bedroom, so I won't forget what I did."

Back in Minnesota, Joan Wirtz can only hope that something positive will come out of the tragedy that claimed the lives of her mother and sister. "If one other teenager can learn from this ordeal," she says, "I hope to God that means that there's one less death."

Teens cause more car crashes than any other age group. To help prevent car crashes by teen drivers and the deaths they cause, more than 40 states have begun

requiring teens to get "graduated licenses." These licenses limit driving privileges for teen drivers until they gain more experience behind the wheel. Graduated licenses may limit teens from driving at night or with other teens in the car. Over time and with a clean record, teen drivers can go on to have full driving rights.

Many people support graduated licenses for teens. Others say these laws are too harsh. What do you think?

PHOTO: © INDEX STOCK IMAGERY

Yes

- **16-year-olds are ten times more likely to crash a car than older drivers.**
- **With graduated licenses, teens learn to drive well without putting people at risk.**

No

- **Most teens are safe drivers. It's unfair to punish all teens because a few are unsafe.**
- **Many teens depend on driving at night to get to and from work.**

The bar graph below compares car safety-related choices teens made in 1995 as compared to 1999. What does the graph show about the choices that teens are making? Why do you think this is so?

Never or Rarely Wears a Seatbelt: **21.7%** 16.4%

Has recently been the passenger with a drunk driver: **38.8%** 31.1%

Has driven after drinking: **15.4%** 13.1%

Source: Centers for Disease Control's Youth Risk Behavior Surveillance: 1999

1995
1999

What's Your Safe Driving IQ?

How much do you know about safe driving? Take this quiz to find out. Write your answers on a separate piece of paper. Then turn the page upside down to see how you did.

1. **At which age is a teen most likely to get into a car accident?**
   a. 16   **b.** 17   **c.** 18

2. **Which percentage of crashes by 16-year-old drivers involve alcohol use?**
   a. 80 percent   **b.** 50 percent   **c.** 15 percent

3. **Which percentage of fatal crashes by 16-year-old drivers involve driver error?**
   a. 82 percent   **b.** 68 percent   **c.** 12 percent

4. **How does the presence of other teens in the car affect the chances of a teen driver having an accident?**
   a. Chances decrease.   **b.** Chances increase.
   c. Chances stay the same.

5. **Which is the safest type of vehicle to drive?**
   a. a sports utility vehicle   **b.** a sports car
   c. a large station wagon

Your Safe Driving IQ Score

1. **a**—Studies show that 16-year-olds, the newest drivers, cause more accidents than 17- and 18-year-olds.

2. **c**—Only 15 percent of 16-year-old drivers killed in car accidents had been drinking. This compares with 32 percent for 17- to 19-year-olds.

3. **a**—82 percent of fatal crashes with 16-year-old drivers involved driver errors, such as speeding and running red lights. The percentage drops to 68 percent for 17- to 19-year-olds.

4. **b**—Having other teens in the car increases the chances of getting into an accident. Drivers will be more distracted, and they may be encouraged by friends to go faster and take dangerous risks.

5. **c**—The larger the car, the safer it is, except in the case of sports utility vehicles. They pose a greater risk of rolling over. With sports cars or performance cars, drivers tend to speed and drive more aggressively.

35

One teen's harrowing story of war, grief, starvation, and survival

4 Escaping Death

by John Kuol, as told to Karen Fanning

John Kuol (pronounced KWAHL) was born in 1983. That same year a brutal civil war broke out in his native country of Sudan, located in northeastern Africa. Four years later, when the fighting reached his village, John was forced to run for his life. The journey would be longer, more frightening, and more brutal than he could have ever imagined.

Over the next 14 years, John became locked in a lonely and heart-breaking struggle for survival. Unfortunately, John's story is just one of many. He belongs to an unusual group of refugees known as the Lost Boys of Sudan, a group of roughly 10,000 boys who became orphans while escaping one of the world's most lethal civil wars. At the age of 17, his nightmarish journey finally ended in the United States. This is his story.

Torn Apart

I was four years old when hundreds of soldiers surrounded my village in southern Sudan. They burned down our homes and killed our relatives, our friends, and our neighbors. I escaped with my parents and two younger brothers and hid, horrified, in the bush.

Soon, though, because of all the chaos, I got separated from my family. I was all by myself, and I was wearing nothing. My feet were bare.

I met up with a small group of people who were walking in the direction of Ethiopia, a neighboring country. They were strangers, but they were kind and decided to help me. After one week, we exhausted our food supply. We ate wild fruit, although it wasn't easy to find. Sometimes, we managed to kill an animal, like an antelope or a buffalo. But most of the time, we survived by scavenging and eating anything that would help us stay alive—leaves, plants, and even roots.

Along the way, lions ambushed us and attacked us. Some of us were killed. Others died of dehydration and thirst. There were also people during the journey who attacked us—robbers. They didn't discriminate in choosing their victims. They killed all kinds of people— both young and old, strong and weak. If you had food, they would steal it without mercy.

Walking to Safety

My country is very arid and hot. During the day, because of the relentless sun and lack of water, we'd rest under the trees. We'd only sleep intermittently, for brief periods of time, because we were so terrified of animals and robbers killing us. We'd walk through the night until it got unbearably hot again. For three months we walked, covering more than 1,000 miles.

In Ethiopia, we managed to find a refugee camp with more than 33,000 other people who had fled Sudan. I was happy because I finally felt protected, but I was also very depressed. I was not only without my family, I had no idea where they were—or if they were alive.

Refugee workers for the United Nations gave us whatever aid they could: food, some clothing, and a tent for housing. Because the camp was overrun with refugees, there weren't enough provisions to go around. Our food rations were enough for us to eat only a bowl of grain, rice, or corn each day, and we got water from a nearby river.

I started school in the camp, but there were no books, pens, or pencils. When I wasn't attending school, I cooked, gathered firewood, and cut down grass for our roofing.

Boys at Camp Kakuma in Kenya survived on just two bowls of grain every two weeks. John Kuol spent eight years here.

I stayed at the camp for four years, until a war broke out in Ethiopia in the winter of 1991. It was time to flee from the violence and chaos once more. On the border of Ethiopia and Sudan, we had to cross the Gilo River. It was wide, freezing cold, and teeming with crocodiles. Luckily, a fisherman took pity and managed to save seven of us. We climbed into his small boat, shivering in the winter air as he rowed us across the river. Some of my friends weren't so lucky. They drowned because the water was so frigid and deep.

Trapped Between Two Wars

We settled in a town called Pochalla on the Ethiopia-Sudan border, stuck between the wars that were still raging in both countries. We stayed there—uncertain about our future—for six months, until United Nations officials came and told us to walk south and find refuge in another country, Kenya. "We'll find a protected place for you," they promised.

The trek took three months. This time, we had clothes and a little food to eat, but no shoes on our feet. It was difficult, but we had no other option or solution. I walked and walked and walked for an unbearably long time. Both my ankles were really swollen, and I had infected sores on my feet. The pain was excruciating. By now, I was using a stick to hobble along. I found a Red Cross clinic, where doctors examined me and said I was extremely malnourished and weak. They said I was a very serious case. Thankfully, the Red Cross was able to drive me and a few other people the remainder of the way to the border of Sudan and Kenya.

In Kenya

We finally arrived at Camp Kakuma in Kenya in August of 1992. This refugee camp would be my home for the next eight years. I lived in a hut with several other people and felt safe at last from the threat of war; but at night, robbers would sneak into the camp and steal our food. I would hear them shooting people. Nighttime was a nightmare, and the fear of an ambush by robbers made it nearly impossible to sleep.

The most important thing the Kenyans gave us was an education: It was a blessing. I studied many subjects, including English, math, science, history, religion, and agriculture. Sadly, some kids didn't have the privilege of going to school because they needed to go search for food.

I never missed school until 1996, when I fell very ill. I was sick for two years. My gums were bleeding; I couldn't manage to eat; my joints were so sore; I was unable to walk.

The doctors told me I was suffering the effects of many years of malnutrition. In Camp Kakuma, we'd get two bowls of corn, rice, or wheat, every two weeks. With so little food to sustain my body, it was nearly impossible to get healthy.

That same year, my brother wrote to me from our village in Sudan to tell me that my parents and baby brother were no longer alive. I don't know whether it was the war or something else that killed them. I was crushed by the news and felt tremendously sad. The people I lived with had become my friends, but they were no substitute for my family.

Promise of America

A few years ago, United Nations workers had told us that we might be resettled as refugees in America. No one in my tribe or my village had ever traveled to America before. I knew nothing about it, except that it was a free country, a peaceful country.

I left Kenya last December never having been on a plane before. At first being suspended in the sky like that made me anxious. I didn't sleep at all because I was so nervous and excited.

When I arrived in Boston, I had never seen snow before. Thoughts were racing through my mind like, "How do people survive here? It's so cold!"

Everything was so new, so amazing. I had never seen a television, a telephone, or a refrigerator. I had never seen tall buildings before. Even the food was different.

Now I've been a resident of America for nine months. I live with my foster father, David Ammerman, and two other African boys: Peter Akol, from Sudan, and Kidani Abadi, from Ethiopia. I'm attending 11th grade at Boston English High School. It's not like the school I was at before. At my new high school, there are lots of books and good teachers and tutors. I study a lot and my backpack is always heavy with books.

It's important for me to get an education. My parents were farmers, and because they weren't educated, life was difficult for them. They suffered a lot. I want to study hard at school so I can become a doctor or a teacher and help people someday.

Missing Home

The best part about being in America is that now I am well protected and I feel safe. I have enough food to eat, and I have good housing.

Still, I am terribly homesick. My brother still remains in Sudan and lives with my uncle in my village. The last time I saw him was in 1987 when I was four years old.

The war is still going on there and my family is still suffering horribly. The hardest part is being away from them. I think of them every day.

For nearly two decades, Sudan's brutal civil war has shattered the lives of people like John Kuol. Since the first shots rang out in 1983, roughly 2 million people have died, and another 4 million have been forced out of their homes.

John's terrifying journey to escape the violence began in his village, Kongor, in Sudan. Sudan is Africa's largest country. John walked more than 1,000 miles from Kongor to an unspecified refugee camp in Ethiopia. In the United States, that would be like walking the entire length of the West Coast, from Seattle, Washington, to San Diego, California.

Refer to the map and answer these questions on a separate piece of paper. when you are done, turn the next page upside down and check your answers

1. **According to the map and the article, Pochalla is a town located on the . . .**
   a. Ethiopia-Kenya border.
   b. Sudan-Ethiopia border.
   c. Sudan-Kenya border.

2. **The southernmost country labeled is . . .**
   a. Kenya.   **b.** Kakuma.   **c.** Ethiopia.

3. **Approximately how many miles is it from Kongor to Kakuma according to the scale of miles provided on the map?**
   a. 1,000 miles   **b.** 500 miles   **c.** 50 miles

4. **About how many miles is it from Kongor to Pochalla?**
   a. 250 miles   **b.** 500 miles   **c.** 1,000 miles

5. **According to the globe inset, Boston, Massachussetts is generally in what direction from Africa?**
   a. northeast   **b.** southeast   **c.** northwest

Sudan is hardly the only country where people are fleeing political unrest and violence. Today, more than 23 million people are considered refugees in places as far-flung as Afghanistan, Iraq, Somalia, Vietnam, Croatia, and the former Yugoslavia. Every year, the United Nations returns thousands of refugees to their homes. But new conflicts are constantly creating new refugees. Look at the line graph below to find out more details.

According to the graph, which year had the least number of refugees?

During which four years was the refugee crisis at its worst?

Overall, does the refugee problem seem to be improving, getting worse or staying the same?

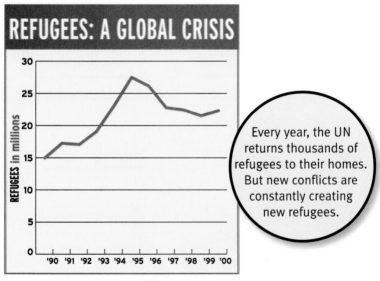

REFUGEES: A GLOBAL CRISIS

Every year, the UN returns thousands of refugees to their homes. But new conflicts are constantly creating new refugees.

SOURCE: UNITED NATIONS HIGH COMMISSIONER FOR REFUGEES

This year, an estimated 80,000 refugees will arrive in the United States. Many will come here without any possessions and without knowing anyone. To adjust to their new lives here, many will need to learn English and learn about American life and customs. Here's how you can help:

- **VOLUNTEER AT A LOCAL RESETTLEMENT AGENCY.** You can help teach refugees English, help them with schoolwork, take them on a tour of your community, or just become an American friend. To find a resettlement agency near you, contact your state office for refugees and immigration.

- **ORGANIZE A DONATION DRIVE.** Newly arrived refugees need clothes, furniture, books, and much more. Check with local churches or a resettlement agency to find out what items they need and how best to collect these items from your community.

- **TEACH OTHER PEOPLE ABOUT REFUGEES.** Invite someone from your state office or a local resettlement agency to speak to your school about refugees in your area. The more people know about refugees and their needs, the more they can help.

PHOTO: © DARREN MCCOLLESTER
LIAISON/GETTY IMAGES

Kelsey Dodge was teased and bullied in middle school. It made her life miserable until she found a way out.

5 Bullying Really Hurts

by John DiConsiglio

The first time Kelsey Dodge encountered bullying was on the school bus in the seventh grade. She was dressed in her customary way, with a long dark skirt, thick jewelry, and flowing black hair spilling down below her shoulders. A girl approached her with a menacing look on her face.

"Are you a witch?" the girl asked with a sneer.

"Of course not," Kelsey said.

"Well, you look like one," the girl said.

Kelsey recognized that her appearance was unusual—most girls at her school favored bleached blonde hair, tank tops, and jeans. So, at first, Kelsey tried to ignore the remarks, but it became increasingly more difficult. Kelsey was a constant target of school bullies, whose veiled threats and caustic comments made her dread stepping foot in the building each morning.

Nowhere to Hide

The teasing started with a rumor, which spread like a virus. On the bus, in the cafeteria, and in the halls of her middle school, Kelsey would hear the same mean-spirited taunts over and over again. Kelsey's classmates hounded her by saying things like: "There goes the witch. Isn't she ugly? Watch out—she'll turn you into a toad."

"People just assumed that, because I wore black, I was a witch," says Kelsey, now 16. "At first I thought, 'Well, this is an annoying bunch of jerks, I'll just ignore them.' But soon the name-calling was everywhere, and I couldn't ignore insults anymore."

For two excruciating years, the students at Kelsey's school maltreated her and made sure every day was a seven-period torture session. The relentless mocking eventually took its toll on Kelsey and her self-esteem. The abuse became so unbearable, Kelsey began to have difficulty sleeping. She couldn't focus or pay attention in class and her grades plummeted. To escape the humiliation, Kelsey even feigned illnesses to stay home from school. Finally, she began seeing a therapist who recommended Kelsey also start taking medicine for depression.

The Real Facts

Bullying—whether it is hitting and shoving, name-calling, or excluding people socially—is a big problem in U.S. schools. How prevalent is the problem? Sixteen percent of students report they have been bullied which, by definition, means they have been the recipients of some form of physical, verbal, or emotional abuse. It doesn't matter if you're a male or a female; if you reside in the city or are from the country. Researchers say bullying occurs in every school.

Sadly, the number of victims is steadily increasing—especially in middle and high schools. "It's definitely on the rise, and on top of that, the bullies are getting meaner and more threatening," says William S. Pollack, an educator at Harvard Medical School who has also authored a book on bullying.

How are kids responding? "Bullied kids tend to suffer from depression more often. Their schoolwork suffers. And they talk about suicide more," says Sue Limber, an expert on bullying. Every day in the United States, 160,000 students skip school to avoid bullying, according to the National Association of School Psychologists. A few victims may even seek violent revenge. A recent study by a branch of the U.S. Secret Service found that in nearly 70 percent of school shootings, the perpetrators felt "persecuted, bullied, threatened, or attacked."

Bullying can also be an indicator of other antisocial behaviors. Research shows that bullies are six times more likely to commit a crime by age 24. "Bullying is a huge problem. Families, schools, and communities have to start taking it seriously," Limber says.

Finding a Way to Survive

In retrospect, Kelsey wishes her classmates and teachers had taken her problem more seriously. Many students seemed totally indifferent to her plight and were reluctant to come to her defense. "I guess they thought that if they stuck up for me they'd be bullied too," Kelsey says.

Kelsey often complained to a guidance counselor who suggested that Kelsey let the bullies know they were hurting her feelings. Kelsey tried that, but it didn't work. Finally, her mom gave her some very pragmatic advice.

"She told me that she knew it hurt a lot. She told me to hold on and try not to let it bother me," Kelsey says.

It took two years, but Kelsey did gradually learn to cope with the teasing. "I'd just say, 'You guys are so immature,' and try to forget about it," she says. "It wasn't easy. I was still hurting inside. Then they saw that they couldn't make me squirm and cry anymore so they got bored and left me alone."

Experts say that Kelsey's approach was the right way to go. According to Limber, cultivating the ability to not react to mean comments deprives the bullies of their desired response. "The bully wants to see you cry," Limber says. "It's no fun for them if you don't react."

Victims of bullying should always enlist assistance from a parent or a teacher whom they trust. Those who witness bullying also have a critical role to play. To be silent is to condone the bully's behavior. "You can be a real hero if you step in and let people know that bullying isn't cool," Limber says.

Kelsey's life has undergone a marked change since she stood up to her bullies. She has an intimate circle of friends now, people who respect her and don't judge her because of her unique style. "I'm glad I didn't let the bullying change the way I am," she says. Also, Kelsey now appreciates the harm that bullying can cause. There's a new girl on the bus who is often teased and Kelsey is always quick to come to her aid. "I know how it feels to be picked on," she says. "I'm never going to sit back and let someone else be treated the way they treated me."

A Bully Apologizes

by Denise Rinaldo

Now a nice guy, Chris once bullied someone like Kelsey. Here's his side of the story.

Chris Morris, 17, is part of his high school security patrol. That's not the kind of thing that a typical bully would sign up to do. That's because Chris isn't a bully—anymore. But back in junior high, he was.

"There was this girl who dressed in black and wore black lipstick and nobody would leave her alone," Chris says. "I picked on her all the time and so did a lot of people. She was in a lot of my classes, and I was always calling her Goth girl and things like that. I didn't really think she took the insults to heart because she never really said anything."

Then, one day, the girl stopped coming to school. Shortly after that, Chris was called to the principal's office. "The principal told me that the girl had left school because people were bullying her and making fun of her. She fingered specific people, and I was one of them."

The meeting with the principal affected Chris deeply. He felt guilty for a long time after the girl left school and says that he would apologize to her if he were ever to encounter her again.

"I'd say I was really, really sorry," says Chris, who's now a senior at Stone Mountain High School in Stephenson, Georgia. "I definitely haven't done anything like that again, and I won't."

Chris says he's reminded of his bullying days when he sees students in school who don't fit in. Even today, Chris isn't sure why bullying happens. "I think that maybe it's that people are insecure with themselves and they look for an easy target—a person who's weaker than they are," he says.

Can you tell the myths from the facts when it comes to bullying? Read each statement then decide if it is true or false. Write your answers on a separate piece of paper. To find out what the experts say, turn the quiz upside down.

1. Bullying is just teasing.

False. While many bullies tease, others use violence and intimidation. Sometimes, being teased can be fun; but being bullied never is. By definition, it's physical abuse (pushing, kicking); verbal abuse (teasing, name-calling, gossip); and emotional abuse (rejecting, humiliating, excluding).

2. Some people deserve to be bullied.

False. No one ever deserves to be bullied. No one "asks for it." Most bullies tease people who are "different," or less powerful, in some way. Being different is not a reason to be bullied.

3. Only boys are bullies.

False. Most bullies are boys, but girls can also be bullies.

4. Bullies will go away if you ignore them.

True & False. Some bullies may go away. But others will get angry and keep bullying until they get a reaction.

5. It's tattling to tell an adult when you're being bullied.

False. It's smart to tell an adult who can help you do something about bullying. It's also smart to tell an adult if you see someone else being bullied.

6. The best way to deal with a bully is by fighting or trying to get even.

False. If you fight with a bully, someone might get hurt. Plus, you might get into trouble for fighting. If you try to get even, you're acting the same way as the bully. And the bully might come after you again to get even with you. Either way only makes things worse.

The Survey Says . . .

Recently, a survey was conducted of 15,686 students in grades 6-10. Nearly 30 percent of them said they had been affected by bullying. The numbers below show how many said they were affected frequently (one or more times a week). The results are divided into responses from male and female students. Were there any differences between the sexes? Look at the double bar graph below to find out.

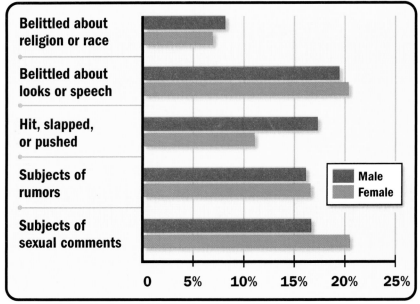

Source: National Institute of Child Health and Human Development

- **How are male and female experiences with bullying different? How are they alike?**

- **How do these numbers compare with you and your friends' experiences in school?**

How to Handle Bullies

ILLUSTRATION: PETER SPACEK

The experts agree: It takes more than one person to put a stop to bullying in school.

Whether you're a victim, an onlooker, or a bully who's ready to make a change, these tips can help you be part of the solution.

1. **Speak Out.** If you see a bully in action, encourage friends or classmates to join you in telling the bully to stop. When a group bands together in support of victim, 90 percent of the time the bullying will stop, experts say.

2. **Be Nice.** Start a program in your school that promotes the message that it's cool to be kind. Lead the campaign by example: Don't laugh at cruel jokes, and don't make them yourself.

3. **Go Beyond Your Group.** Reach out to students who don't seem to fit in. You'll be helping someone, plus you may make a new friend.

4. **Use Your Power for Good.** Are you popular? If so, that's great. Use your popularity to bring fellow students together and to discourage "cliques."

5. **Ask For Help.** Whether you're a bully, victim, or bystander, you don't have to try to solve all your problems alone. Talk to a trusted adult (a parent, teacher, or school counselor). If the first person you go to can't help you, keep trying until you find someone who can.